Life
In
America

A Short Story By: Cruz Whites

I dedicate this book to my Grandpa Cob Hitchon. He always tells me and my sister great stories, he always said that when I become a famous writer I will have to dedicate my books to him. That is exactly what I decided to do. Here's to you King Papa!

- Cruz Whites

July

July 19th

Today is my first day in America, the Country and the Continent. I am proudly sitting on my very own bed in my very own room. I am so happy to have my very own space. Not only that, but I love looking around and seeing only my stuff- not that Moma and Doda's stuff was in the way, it was just there and not mine.

This journal seems so soft, I enjoy touching the cover and the soft pages.

I am so anxious to go around tomorrow and say hello to everyone. My Moma told me, "If anyone judges you by your **Jewish** clothes or your German-English accent, just leave." Tomorrow will be interesting.

July 20th

Today was both exciting and hurtful. **The exciting part** is that I made an African-English friend named Zaara. She said that Marie was a very delightful name and that she was also born in England, but her parents were born in **Kenya.** I told her that I was born in **England**, but both my parents were born in Germany. The hurtful part was that a woman with a heavy German accent told me to "leave my German family alone." She clearly did not want me near her family. But since she had such a heavy accent it sounded like, "keteve budi **German** vejamily atone" She also translated it to German in case I didn't speak English, so it sounded like this: "Lass meine deutsche Familie in Ruhe."

Later that day I asked Zaara to translate what she said to me in Afrikaans. It sounded like this: “Laat my Duitse gesin met rus”. Nazzi Pa even translated it into French for me. It’s appeal was even worse in French: “Laisse my famille allemande seule.”

July 21st

School starts on September 4th. I am really nervous. I speak English, but I recorded myself, so when I say “My name is Marie” it sounds like “Ji vame dis Cadie”. It rhymes because my German-English accent has the “smell of rhyme” like Moma and Naja say. But when I talked to Zaara about it, she said nαt to worry because her Moma was the Principal, and she would make sure that Zaara and I were in the same class for 4th grade this year. She said she would help me out. I thanked Zaara, but I wished that Zaara would nαt need to help me. The way Zaara and I talk is by talking in my second language, French (German is my first language and English is my third language), so my heavy accent does nαt get in the way.

July 22nd

Today came with terrible news! Zaara is moving to Africa to live with her Aunt Tora and Uncle Jwe. Zaara's parents died! They were shot dead by an American man when they were walking down Main Street. Zaara said the police have a photo from the street camera but no lead.

I no longer have a friend to protect me, to talk to me and to believe in me. I no longer understand America. This world is endlessly cruel to everyone, from when **Hitler** took my Grandpa to when a selfish American man killed Mr. and Mrs. Ketayan (Zaara's parents).

July 23rd

Today I had Nazzi Pa and Paja (my grandfathers) take me downtown, so I could discover this American man and turn him into the police because what he had done was terribly wrong. (I had to take my grandfathers because my grandmothers were decorating the house and my parents were at work. I also knew my grandfathers could keep a secret). I had cut out the photo of the man from the

Miradero Press and glued it to my clipboard so I would be able to reference it. Nazzi Pa and Paja already knew what I was doing; I had told them the plan on the way down- I had even bought them an ice cream! Any man that looked suspicious and looked like the sketch, I questioned. In the end, I had questioned fifteen men and gotten their first and last name. Tomorrow I will have to do the hard part.

July 24th

The hard part was what I did today. I looked up all fifteen names in the public phone book in our Town Square. I got the addresses of each man I questioned yesterday, and then went to each house and questioned every man's wife. Each time, I repeated the same question: "Do you know anything about who killed Mr & Ms. Ketayan?"

Every woman said "no" and that their husband had not shot down Mr. and Mrs. Ketayan.

One woman said that I should ask Mrs. Lucy Burr at *200257 Walking Drive*. Suddenly, as if she recognized what she had said, she slammed the door in my face. As if

that was not enough, she then closed the blinds with a frightened look in her eyes.
The woman who had told me about Mrs. Lucy Burr was named Mary-Ann Hopkins. I wrote her name and her address on my clipboard.

July 25th
Today I went to meet this Lucy Burr. I told her that Ms. Mary-Ann Hopkins had said to ask her. Mrs. Burr said that her husband had left an hour before Mr. and Mrs. Ketayan were killed. She said he had not come back yet. The last thing she said sent a horrible shiver throughout me. Finally, she said that he had left with his **rifle** and his **revolver**. When I asked her if her husband (Mr. Zack Burr) liked to hunt animals, Mrs. Burr said that her husband had never actually gone hunting in his life. I thanked Mrs. Lucy Burr and left feeling crazed.

July 26th
Today I asked Nazzi Pa (since he knew the most about American history,) if Burr was a name he knew in

American history. Nazzi Pa said that, "Yes, I knew of Aaron **Burr**. Aaron Burr was a historical figure that killed **Alexander Hamilton** in a **duel** after the American Revolution. Aaron Burr was also **Thomas Jefferson**'s first Vice President in the two four year terms that Jefferson had served as president." Suddenly it registered in my brain that Aaron Burr killed the man on the American ten dollar bill. I did some research and found out that Alexander Hamilton was also an immigrant, but he immigrated from the West Indies. It says that he was Secretary of The Treasury and a great soldier of the Revolutionary War.

I decided to make a pot of lemon tea to bring to Mrs. Burr. Once it was done, I went to her place. I wanted to find out if Mrs. Burr knew if Zack was a relative of Aaron, which he is.

Mrs. Burr said, "My husband was some type of relative to Aaron Burr." I believe that I shuddered when she said that, but it was so quick I do not know if I did.

July 27th

Last night, when I came home I told Nazzi Pa what Mrs. Burr had said. He told me that we should go see the police about it and see if they could help us. Nazzi Pa believes that the police were our only hope to find someone to help us.

Today, Zaara said that she was moving to Africa in 5 days. She asked if I could help her pack up her closet and book collection. Zaara loves books so much she never shows up without a book. She always likes to give me recommendations, and they are always so good! Then at about 1:30 Nazzi Pa called and said it was time to go to the Police station. I told Zaara goodbye and went with Nazzi Pa to the police station. We went to the police station on Main Street. When we got there two British-looking men were at the front desk. I went ahead and told them what I was there for and the information I had gathered. I gave them my name and all the facts. But as I started stating why I had looked into this, I noticed that the men were giving each other looks. The looks were almost saying, "This girl is talking nonsense; she has no information." Right when I saw those looks I became infuriated. I whispered to Nazzi Pa and told him that we had to leave. So he went and told the men that our mid-afternoon snack was ready, and we had to go. They did not seem to understand, but I did not care. I walked out of there and told Nazzi Pa what had happened. When we got home, the news spread between my grandparents about what had happened. My Naja said that what they did was completely wrong. My Paja said that they should be taught a lesson, he volunteered to do it, but I said it was okay.

Finally, my Nazzi Na came and told me that not every soul is full of happiness like mine. She said that Hitler was also an evil man who had no kindness either. She said that I was lucky to have Nazzi Pa, Paja and Naja with me because their souls are full of happiness.

July 28th

Today me and Nazzi Pa went to a second police station where a young woman was sitting at the front desk. I went up to her and said, "My name is Marie Altergott. I am 10 years old and I have something to tell you." She said, "I am Kamalla Singh and I would like to hear the case, so please go along and tell me." I told her my evidence- names of people and why I researched and did all the work for the case. Ms. Singh took notes the whole time. When I was done, she turned to me and told me that she would need my address to contact me if my information was correct. I then turned to Nazzi Pa, and he gave the house information to Ms. Singh. I was very nervous then. I was worried that if the information was wrong, I would look like I made it all up. I was also nervous that if I was right I would look like some Detective Genius.

August

August 1st

I did not write for the last couple of days because I was busy taking care of my new dog! My parents saw that I was so sad that Zaara was moving. They decided I needed a dog to make me happy. We were going to get a German Shepherd, but then I saw Mara and I knew I needed to get her instead. She is a mini goldendoodle. Her name stands for Maravillosa in Spanish, but I call her Mara for short. Sadly Zaara left for Kenya, Africa, today on the ten o'clock plane out of Seattle, Washington. Mara keeps me happy and busy. I walk her three times a day on a regular basis. We take a walk before breakfast, then one before lunch, and finally one before dinner- and sometimes one after dinner.

August 3rd
Mara has been having trouble sleeping a lot, so I read when she sleeps and walk her when she's awake.

One day, when I was reading in our small house library, the doorbell rang. I heard Nazzi Pa and Paja- who had been playing Boggle- get the door.

About a minute later, Nazzi Pa came in and told me to come into the living room. Sitting in the living room was Ms. Singh. Mara had woken up and was sniffing Ms. Singh. After I had pulled Mara away from Ms. Singh, I asked her, "Ms. Singh, why are you here?" She told me that she had researched the case and that all the evidence points to Zack Burr. But there was no hard evidence. The most exciting thing she said was... would I like to spend a day with her doing research on the case? I said, "Yes!" My grandparents agreed.

Finally, I told my parents what I had been doing and asked them if I could go with Ms. Singh tomorrow. They were both about to say no, but my grandparents stood up for me. I better get to sleep now because I have a big day of detective work ahead of me. But before I go, I want to write something:

I am very proud of myself. I knew I could do it. I hope I have good luck tomorrow.

August 4th

I just got home from working with Ms. Singh. I have great news! We went to interview Mrs. Burr. Mrs. Burr claimed she did know her husband had murdered Zaara's parents. We now had evidence that Zack Burr had done it! But the one thing we did not know was where Zack Burr was. Mrs.

Burr said that she and her husband owned a cabin up in the mountains near Snow Town, which was about fifty or so miles from Miradero (where we live). Ms. Singh is coming tomorrow with her other police friend to pick me up so we can go up to see if he is in the cabin in Snow Town. In the meantime, the police are moving Mrs. Burr to custody for two reasons:

1. If Zack Burr found out what Mrs. Burr did he might hurt her, and
2. She **knew** about the plot.

I have no clue what tomorrow has in store for me; and maybe, just maybe, another secret about Zack Burr will be uncovered. I am so nervous that if we find him that he will be hostile, but I was told that I would be safe.

August 5th

I have total goose bumps. I just got back from helping Ms. Singh and her police friend Ms. Joyce. Zack Burr was **not** in the cabin, but there was a coded note in Morse code:

.... . .-.. .-.. ---, .-.. ..- -.-. -.--

.. ..-. -.-- --- ..- .- .-. . .-. . .- -.. .. -. --. - .... -. --- -

. .. .- -- -. --- .-- .. -. ... . .- - - .-.. . , .-- .- ... . -. --. -

--- -. . .. .-- .. .-.. .-.. -... . ... - .- -.-- .. -. --. .- - - .... . .-

.--. .- .-. - -- . -. - ..- -. - .. .-.. .- ..- --. ..- ... - --... - ....

- .... . -. .. .-- .. .-.. .-.. -... . .-.. . .- ...- .. -. --. - .... . -.-.

--- ..- -. - .-. -.-- .- -. -.. --. --- .. -. --. - --- . -. --. .-..

.- -. -.. . .. . --- .--. . - --- -- . . - -.-- --- ..- - .... . .-. .

--- -. - .... . .---- ----- - .... .

-.-- --- ..- .-. .... ..- ... -... .- -. -.. --.. .- -.-. -.-

It translated to :

Hello, Lucy

If you are reading this note I am now in Seattle, Washington. I will be staying at the apartment until August 7th then I will be leaving the country and going to England. I hope to meet you there on the 10th.

Your Husband Zack.

Seattle is not very far from here since Miradero is right on the state border between Washington and Oregon. Ms. Joyce will come to pick me up tomorrow at 9:30 a.m. because Ms. Singh is leaving tonight to get the address from Mrs. Burr and maybe catch Zach with some evidence.

I hope Ms. Singh finds some information because the sooner we catch him will make me feel better, and it will also make Zaara feel better. Good night.

August 6th

Ms. Singh is missing. Ms. Joyce and I have no clue where she has gone. We both guess that Zack Burr caught her and is now probably going to have her promise to not say anything, or else he might hurt her. Again, there was a message to us. It was in Morse code again. Here is what it looked like:

Dear Police,

.. -.- -. --- .-- -.-- --- ..- .- .-. . ..-. --- .-.. .-.. --- .-- ..

-. --. -- . - .... --- ..- --. .... .. -.. --- -. --- - -.- -. ---

.-- .... --- .-- -.-- --- ..- --. --- - .- .-.. .-.. - .... -.

..-. --- .-. -- .- - .. --- -. --- -. -- . , ...- ...- . -. ---

.-- - .- -.- . -. -- ..., ... -. --. .... .- -. -.. - --- --. . - ....

. .-., -.. . -.-. .. .--. .... . .-. - .... -.-. --- -.. . .- -. -.. --.

. - .... . .-. -... .- -.-. -.-. : :020:015 060901404 013019. 019090708 07015 023080501805 :020:0805 0150160501801 09019 01902101407.0906 025015021

0101805 014015:020: :020:080501805 02025 :020:0805 :020:0901305 :020:0805 0301201503011 03080901305 0i 01:020: 014090708:020: 015014 0102107. 0i 0190805 02309012012 0601012012 06018015013 :020:0805 0801012012.

It was Alpha numeric code, and said something about getting Ms. Singh from where the opera is sung. It also said if the police are not there when the clock chimes 8 tomorrow night, Ms. Singh will fall from a hall. I will not be going tomorrow, but Ms. Joyce and her partner Mr. Joyce will go tomorrow to catch Zack in the act and get Ms. Singh back. They said that there are two reasons why Zack Burr is putting Ms. Singh in the Opera Hall.

1. He used to work at the Opera House.
2. Ms. Singh's name is pronounced (Si-ng) like the word "sing", so it kind of makes sense.

Tomorrow I would not have been allowed to go anyway, because it is Doda's birthday tomorrow. We are all going to go to this English food restaurant called British Bites. Zaara said she has gone there before and the menu is great. She said that they copy the English recipes perfectly. Well, now I have to get a good night's rest for tomorrow.

August 7th

Today was Doda's birthday, and it was great (except for everyone throwing up because the British Bites meal had fish in it, and we are all allergic to fish). I called up Zaara to let her know, and she laughed. She said she had no idea we were allergic to fish and then apologized—well, she apologized after she was done laughing! She said that being my friend was a great thing because I always made her laugh, and always contacted her. Not only that, but she also said that I am her Best Friend From Afar.

When we went to lunch at British Bites, Mara came along, and we walked her around the town. On Towns Main St. we found a great bookstore called Towne Books. We went inside and each got a book. I got a book called "For Freedom: The Story of a French Spy". It takes place in World War II. That was the war where Hitler took my Paja and put him in a concentration camp. Nazzi Pa met him there. You know what, I am going to tell you the story of my family's history. It is very interesting. First, let me put in a Nazzi Pa quote: "The story of a family is a story of life, and a story about our family is like jumping off a cliff without a parachute: You never know what happens next. All you know is you will survive and preserve the Altergott family story."

My Family's Story:

My grandfather (Paja) is Jewish and his real name is Abraham David. When my grandfather was 22 in the beginning of World War II, his family lived in Germany. One day there was a firm knock at the door. The door was kicked open a few seconds later. The Nazis came in and took Paja and his father. Paja's mother and sister had died in the Hindenburg Disaster, but Paja and his Doda were already off the Hindenburg because they were being followed by the Nazis and had to get away. They took Paja and my great grandpa to a concentration camp. Supposedly, my great-grandfather had been a spy for the French for a time, so the Nazis shot and killed him when they found out.

After a week, a new guard was posted outside the jail Paja was in. Suddenly, the other Jewish people in the camp started disappearing. About eight days after Paja was put in the concentration camp, the guard approached him and asked Paja to follow him. Paja did as he was told, and the guard showed him a small opening in the gate. He told Paja to go through that hole and never come back. Paja escaped from Germany and went to Denmark for two years. When he was there he met Naja; another Jewish person who was also German. Her name was Aria. They fell in love and after the war got married as well as moved back to the house that Paja's family had once lived in. Then they had my Moma. Her name is Mila.

About twenty years later, the guard from the concentration camp knocked on Paja and Naja's door. He told Paja that Paja owed him something, since the guard had freed him from the camp. Paja thought about it for five years, and finally he came up with something. His daughter (my Moma) had fallen in love with the guard's son, Hans Altergott. The guard, Stefan Altergott (also known as Nazzi Pa), gave his son to them. Paja gave Moma his blessing, and three years later Hans (also known as Doda) and Moma got married. Two years later, Nazzi Pa and his wife Emilia moved to England. Paja, Naja, Moma, and Doda went with them. About a month later I was born. I loved living in England, but finally Moma and Doda and both of my grandparents decided that I deserved to grow up in America. They wanted me to live the American dream. Once we came to America I started writing in my notebook and writing about the American dream of life. When we first got here, I did not think there was such a thing as the "American dream" since Zaara's parents were killed and Ms. Singh was taken. But as I write my family's story just now, I see that the American dream is about freedom—not about dream homes and all that stuff. Well, here comes Nazzi Pa and Paja to read me a story. I have to go now.

August 8th

Ms. Joyce and Mr. Joyce came over today with a special guest… It was Ms. Singh! They had found her tied to the wall in the back of the Opera House, but they did not see

Zack Burr. (So annoying.) Ms. Singh had drawn a sketch of Zack Burr, so we now know what he looks like. He has brown hair, green eyes, is about 6 feet, skinny, and American-looking. There was another coded message waiting for us. They found Ms. Singh at the Seattle Opera with another note in Morse code:

.. .- -- --. --- -. . .. .- -- --. --- -. . .. .- -- --. --- -. .

.. -. . -. --. .-.. .- -. -.. .. ..-. -.-- --- ..- ..-. .. -. -.. -- .

-.-- --- ..- .-- .. .-.. .-.. -... . .-.. ..- -.-. -.- -.--. - .... . . -.

--. .-.. .. ..--. --- .-.. .. -.-. . -.. --- -. --- - ..-. .- ...-

--- .-. -.-- --- ..-. ... --- -... .- ....- -- -... ..- --. .- -.

-.. .- .... .- .--. .--. -.-- .- ..- --. ..- ... - - --- -.-- --- ..-.

It means this: *I am gone I am gone I am gone in England if you find me you will be lucky. The English police do not favor you. So bah humbug and a happy August to you.*

Ms. Joyce was stunned, but Paja and Naja had an idea. Naja and Paja's nephew was the chief of the English police. Their nephew loves them so much and will do anything for them. So, before I came in here to write in my journal, Ms. Joyce called up Elijah (Naja and Paja's nephew) and filled him in on the case. Elijah promised that if there was any trace of Mr. Burr, Elijah would ship him over here. I hope they catch him. I also cannot wait to put him to justice. Good night.

August 9th

Ms. Joyce came and asked me how I found out about Ms. and Mr. Burr. I told her that Ms. Mary-Ann Hopkins had told me and then seemed to regret it. Ms. Joyce decided that we should both go and see what Ms. Hopkins knew. Later today, we got to go ask Ms. Hopkins some questions. She said that she had been good friends with Mrs. Burr until Mrs. Burr stole her best china set, which had been a family heirloom going down for 24 generations. Ms. Joyce said that Mrs. Burr was now in jail, and Ms. Joyce would get the china set back to Ms. Hopkins. Ms. Hopkins thanked her and asked if there were any other questions she could answer. We asked her about Mr. Burr. Ms. Hopkins had grown up with Zack Burr, and she claimed he had never liked the idea of African-Americans holding any sort of power. Ms. Hopkins and Mr. Burr were no longer friends because Ms. Hopkins had married an

African-American. I just thought that Mr. Burr did not like Ms. Ketayan because she was principal of a school, plus Mr. Ketayan was head police chief here in Miradero.

August 10th

Today, we called up Elijah. When we were on the phone we heard a voice say, "Elijah, are you almost done? We have to go steal that golden diamond." Then we heard another voice say, "Burr, Elijah's on the phone, be quiet. If he was on the phone with his aunt we would all be discovered." My Naja was very, very upset to know that Elijah was helping Burr rather than his own family. I do not understand why Naja is upset; I never trusted Elijah. He was annoying and never seemed to like me. I actually thought of an equation: Elijah + Burr = TROUBLE! Ms. Joyce claimed she had a plan about getting England to help us. She said that when we meet tomorrow she will tell me her plan.

August 11th

Today Ms. Joyce told me the wackiest plan that I have ever heard of. Ms. Joyce had contacted President Clinton (The President of the United States of America!) to see if he could help get England to help us. Ms. Joyce used to be in the Secret Service protecting Ronald Reagan, George H.W. Bush, and President Clinton for one year (!). Then Ms. Joyce decided she wanted a different job, plus that was when she met her husband.

Tomorrow I am going to call Zaara to tell her what I have found out. I know Zaara will be ecstatic to hear everything, especially since it is finding out who killed her own parents. I just got a letter from her today. Zaara's letter sounds like a little autobiography since she moved to Africa. It was full of details and really good. Zaara had always been a good writer, but going to Africa made her seem like an even better writer—probably because I gobble up every word she writes.

Her address is 4546 Casablanca Ave.

Agadir Morocco 80000.

Her letter said,

Dear Marie,

Hallo vriend (means hello friend) How are you? I am settling in, but it is not like home and no one is as friendly as you!

I was wondering if you know who your teacher is? School just started and my teacher is Ms. Buzaglo (She farts every day when the hour clock ticks! The principal said that she just has allergies, but I doubt it. Who has allergies and farts when the hour clock ticks?) School is so different. They give so much homework! But my aunt always helps me. She is great at math. When she went to college in the US (where you are), she got a part-time job as an accountant. She teaches me new ways to do math and makes it very, very fun! I knew she would be of some help because my parents used to tell me stories about her going to the US for college and how that inspired them to move here with me when I was 6.

I heard that Finland does not give homework. Isn't that absurd? It sounds easy and fun! Two of my favorite things. My aunt says that homework gives you great grades because you are constantly learning new things, even at home.

I was wondering the day after you got this letter if you could call me?! Do a collect call to Zaara Ketayan from Marie Altergott. I would love it if you could answer all my questions because they are very important. We have to do a report on a person that we know, and I chose you, so I will need a lot of information for my report. I will let my aunt know you will call around lunchtime so she can put you on hold until I get home. At my school, they let you go home for lunch and then go back to school if you need homework help. I do not, so I just eat lunch and stay at home. My neighbor needs extra help in school so he goes back. I think it is because he always brings a book and reads when he is supposed to be taking notes.
My aunt also makes the best lunch! It is always healthy and delicious. We live in the best neighborhood that has a fruit garden where I go every afternoon. Also, the internet is terrible here. The only thing that really works is collecting phone calls. Absurd huh? This is when I wish I lived in the US again with Mother and Father. But we do not always get what we want. Bye!

Your Best Friend From Afar (Africa!) Zaara!
The letter is so well punctuated! Well, good night, journal!

August 12th
Today I woke up with a small cough. I had some cough drops, but I am still coughing. Moma said, "You might just have a small dose of the flu." If so, it will hopefully be over by tomorrow.

I *did* call Zaara. It was so comforting to hear her voice. I answered all her questions, plus I sent a letter today asking her questions. She said that once she gets the letter she will call me the next day and answer *all* of my questions. I told her, "I have a lot of questions!"
She said, "It is okay. I love talking to you; it brings me so much joy to hear my best friend's voice."
Well, I am tired and my throat itches, so I am going to sleep with hopes that I will feel better tomorrow.

August 15th

I have been sick with the flu and resting for the last three days. In England, they had peaches around this time of the year and Moma would make peach juice, peach jam, peach noodles, and peach chunks. Sadly we do not have any peaches but my moma made me something called Top Ramen (it was chicken). It was quite good. I am having it for dinner later tonight. I do believe that American foods taste good, so I will try some more when I am no longer sick. But now I must take a rest.

I am now done with my rest now. Ms. Joyce just came by and gave me some news.

Today Ms. Joyce got a call from President Clinton, and he got help from the Minister of England. England knows about all the illegal acts that Burr has been doing. Ms. Singh is also searching Burr's house and seeing what she can find out. (She also found Ms. Hopkins's china set and returned it.) Ms. Joyce has been spending her days interviewing Ms. and Mr. Hopkins to see what they know so far about Mr. and Mrs. Burr. She made a copy of the notes and gave them to me. My copy is pasted below. I also put some of my own comments in parentheses.

- *Ms. Hopkins grew up with Mr. Burr (she says he was always a pain)*
- *Mrs. Burr once stole Ms. Hopkins twenty-four generation china set (so mean)*
- *Mr. Burr hates African-Americans, especially when they hold power. Mr. Hopkins is African-American. (Mr. Burr should **not** judge people the way he does, that is exactly what Hitler did!)*
- *Mr. and Ms. Hopkins have one child named April. She once caught Burr stealing something and she got a medal for catching him, but then Burr must have some friends in the police department. We know this because he never showed up in jail. (when I heard that, it reminded me of something from the TV show Carmen Sandiego)*
- *April now lives in England and works for the police system. (she did not work for Elijah)*

Well, I have to sit right here on my bed and eat my dinner. I will read my book For Freedom and eat my dinner here. Au revoir.

August 16th

Today all I did was read, except when Ms. Singh came over, and she told me what we know so far in the case. So far we know that Mr. Burr and Elijah are working together, and they are pulling off a bunch of different capers. Also, the police, Ms. Singh, and Ms. Joyce are trying to find out where Burr is staying in England. Mrs. Burr refuses to give us answers about this. She said she doesn't know about any house in England, but Ms. Singh and Ms. Joyce tell me not to believe her. Mr. John Major (The Minister of England) called me today to tell me that they have a house registered under Aaron Zack. (Mr. Burr might not be as smart as I give him credit for.) They told me that they will search the house tomorrow and will call to tell me what information they have so far.

My birthday is in 10 days.

Since I am sick and can not go anywhere, Nazzi Na and Naja are watching out for me as Moma, Doda, Nazzi Pa and Paja are going out and looking for my birthday presents. I will be turning 10, so it is SUCH a big deal for me and my family.

Also, Zaara called and said that the letter might take too long to get to her, so she had me ask her the questions today and I did. I did have a lot of questions. It took a whole hour for me to ask them and for Zaara to answer them. Well, Naja and Nazzi Na have come in to play a quick game with me before bed. Good night.

August 17th

I feel like I am getting over the flu (pretty much). Ms. Singh came over *again, and* she told me the plan she had scheduled for us to do on the 20th. We will go to see Mr. Hopkins. He will come with us to the police station, where we will question the police guards that were rude to me. Ms. Singh thinks they might know something and that they did not say, and they might have been paid to keep their mouth shut and ignore everyone who tried to come in with evidence against Zack Burr. I did ask Ms. Singh why he would pay the other police officers but not Ms. Singh. She said she did not know, but she would think about it tonight and let me know tomorrow.

Mr. John Major called and said, "They searched the house and there was evidence that Zack Burr owns it! That is where he keeps all the supplies and everything else that would be illegal to have in the U.S.A." I asked if they saw any trace of when he was last there. Mr. Major explained that the fingerprints look quite fresh, which means he was probably there last night. There was also another fingerprint which belonged to Elijah, which means Elijah was there last night, which means trouble.

August 19th

I did not write yesterday because I was recovering from the flu. I had a relapse, so I was stuck in bed for a couple more days. Nobody else in my family got the flu, though, I wonder where I got it from.

Ms. Joyce came by today and Ms. Singh came by yesterday. But first let me tell you that Naja, Paja, Nazzi Pa and Nazzi Na are taking me out for dinner tonight to celebrate school starting even though school does not start till early September. I am supposed to be getting dressed (but I already have gotten dressed, so I am waiting for them to come get me).

Ms. Joyce came by today and told me that Zack Burr now has a criminal record in America and England. That means that when he goes to court, the court will look at the criminal record and decide how long he should be in jail for. I hope he goes to jail and does not get out until his 100th birthday. Ms. Joyce said that when they bring Zack Burr to court they will have me testify, which means I will have to talk about the case and talk about the harm Burr has done.

When Ms. Singh came yesterday, she told me that the plan that we will do with Mr. Hopkins is happening tomorrow. She said that she talked with Mr. Hopkins, and he likes the idea. I have never met Mr. Hopkins, but he sounds very nice. Naja and Nazzi Na have insisted that they come along when we go do the interrogation with the other police officers. Ms. Singh also said that she had thought about it and the reason that Zack did not ask her to work for him is that:

1. She is a daughter of two African immigrants

2. She is a woman.
Sorry, I have to go now. Bye.

August 20th
I just got home from working with Ms. Singh, Mr. Hopkins, Naja, and Nazzi Na. We found out that the police officers were helping Zack. They were helping him because he promised them a lot of money. But there is even greater news: Ms. Joyce just caught Zack Burr in the middle of India. We called up President Clinton and the minister of England. The time to get from India to here is about 19 hours and 50 plus minutes. It is 8 p.m. now, so they should arrive around 3:50 p.m. here tomorrow. Ms. Joyce just got on the plane, so my calculations should be correct. I will write tomorrow right after everything happens. Well, I am so tired, so now I am going to sleep.

August 21st
Today I came face to face with the man who killed Zaara's parents. He argued and said a lot of bad words. Ms. Joyce just shoved him into the cell, and then we went to discuss

a court date. Well, I did not go with Ms. Singh, Ms. Joyce, and Moma; but Ms. Joyce did tell me the date. Zack Burr is set to go to court on September 3rd, which is thirteen days from today. I will get to present the case. Since my Doda is a lawyer, he will be our lawyer. Zack Burr's lawyer is some English guy named Noah Smith. I hear he is not a very good lawyer. The only reason Zack Burr got Noah Smith as a lawyer was because the rest of the lawyers said no. They knew they would not win the case, and then they would go down as terrible lawyers for fighting for Burr.

Doda is very excited to do his first American court case. He is also very nervous. He has been studying the dictionary (because, like me, we speak German and English mixed when we are talking) and planned out what he is going to say. I have told him not to worry, but he never seems to hear me. Nazzi Pa and Nazzi Na try to calm him down too, but it does not work for them either. I think Doda should at least listen to them since they are his parents, but I saw that he did not stop worrying even after Nazzi Pa and Nazzi Na told him to stop worrying too. Well, anyway, I am so tired, so I am going to sleep now.

August 25th

I have not been able to write for four days because there has been so much absurd preparation for the court case. Everyone has been so busy and every night I have been so tired that I just fall asleep once my body hits the bed. One time I almost fell asleep in the bathtub! I was taking a quick bath, and I was so tired I fell asleep for ten minutes. Eventually Naja went in to check on me, and I was asleep, so she woke me up. We laughed a lot. But anyway, Ms. Joyce said that I should write in my journal. I decided to do as she said. I am going to tell you what happened the past four days I did not write.

On the 22nd, I got to call Zaara and interview her for the judgeship. That took two hours. Then I had to take all that information and write a report about the information I gathered; which took so long I do not know how people can do that for a living.

On the 23rd, I got to go with Ms. Joyce and Ms. Singh to clean out the Burr house to see if there was anything to use as evidence. We found Ms. Hopkins's china set. I returned it to Ms. Hopkins. She was so grateful she gave me some tea to take home.

We also found phσtos of Mr. Ketayan and Msr. Ketayan. There was also a *How to Hack* book.

Yesterday my family, Ms. Singh, and Ms. Joyce held a six-hour meeting in the front room of our house. We talked about our plan for the 3rd, as well as just to talk. I slept for three and read for three hours.

So that is a whole summary of the last four days. But today all I did was read and look at recipes for my birthday tomorrow. I decided that I will write tomorrow and explain every detail. Well, my hand hurts, and I am tired, so I am going to go to bed. Good night.

August 26th

Today was so exciting!

From 8:45-9:45, me and my grandparents watched a show called "Hawaiian Life". It was so good. In the show the people sold these houses to people in **Hawaii**! We have always wanted to go to Hawaii. My family actually calls the Hawaiian Islands the Vacation Islands. We want to go to

Hawaii really badly, and the show made me want to go even more.

Then, after that, we had a Full English Breakfast. (We only have Full English Breakfasts on someone's birthday.) It was delicious.

Then we all played a game called Scrabble, and I won all five rounds.

Then we all took a break and read books.

After that we had chicken sandwiches for lunch.

Then we played and ran around. After that, we had dinner, which was Franzbrötchen, a German cinnamon bun, and Moma made pizza! Zaara told me that pizza is a big deal in America.

Then we opened presents. I actually got a new book called The Vanderbeekers of 141st Street.

August 27th

Today we called Elijah and Ms. Singh taped the call (which means we recorded the call in case he admitted anything) for any useful information. We called him up to tell him we had caught Burr and that we wanted to know why he had joined Burr. He told us to keep whatever he told us on the down low. Then Elijah informed us that Burr was planning on stealing (before we caught him!) a bunch of important artifacts from around the world. He told us that Burr's plan was to sell each artifact for a billion extra dollars than it really cost.

After the phone call, Ms. Singh told us that we would have to go to Burr's warehouse to see if there was anything that proved it. Ms. Singh taught me about something called "He said, she said." Which means that you can not rely on everything someone says Ms. Singh said we can not trust everything Elijah said. She is going to go to England with **me, Nazzi Pa, and Moma** to check out Burr's warehouse.

Ms. Joyce came by today and told me that she questioned Burr, and he told her that he was stealing Venus, a special type of gem in India.

Now I have to pack. We will leave tomorrow to go search Zack Burr's warehouse.

August 28th

I am on the plane, and we are about fifteen minutes away from arriving in England! I am excited to be home even for just a day! We will search Burr's warehouse when we get there, then we will go to sleep, and then wake up. Then we will go to India to return the jewel Burr stole and search his condo there. We will fly home late at night on the 30th, and arrive home early in the morning on the 31st. I have been reading and playing with my Rubik's Cube on the plane so far. We are now descending and landing at the airport. Moma said to stop writing and write tomorrow. Bye!

August 29th

Today we searched Zack Burr's warehouse, and... There was evidence! He had photos of Zaara's old house and a camera full of photos of Mr. and Mrs. Ketayan! But most importantly, there were photos of Mr. Ketayan and Mrs. Ketayan on street cameras. Yes! Yes! Evidence!

We are already getting ready for bed. We leave at 5:30 a.m. tomorrow to get on the plane for India. I am so tired. Good night.

August 30th

Paja and Naja called today to say that last night Mara went into my room and when I was not there and howled. When we get home tomorrow, I am going to call Zaara and ask her some questions about how she is feeling, and ask her if she could call the judge on the 2nd to give her perspective. But today, when we all searched Zack's apartment in India, there was nothing there. We returned the gem to the police, and they were very grateful. We are getting on the plane right now to go home. I am so tired from all the searching we did. I cannot wait to be home, with Naja, Paja, and Nazzi Na. Moma says she misses her parents, but she trusts Nazzi Pa. I am so tired, I just yawned three straight times in a row. Plus we are getting on the plane, so I have to stop writing and maybe, maybe, take a nap on the plane.

August 31st

Today we got home, and Mara was so happy. I took her on an hour walk with both of my grandparents and filled them in on everything. Nazzi Pa loved talking about the case. I was like his own little detective.

Then I called Zaara and I asked her some questions that Ms. Joyce said to ask her. The questions were: When Zaara's parents got murdered, how did she process it all? How did she feel? Did she want to move in with her aunt and uncle in Africa so quickly—or she just didn't have any other choice? Zaara said that when she processed it was not hard to believe. Her parents used to tell her that being African, being smart, and having great jobs put their lives in jeopardy every day. Zaara said she felt mad and nothing else. She was mad at the world, at Burr, and at the police (except Ms. Joyce and Ms. Singh). And for the last question, she said that her doda grew up with five brothers but only one survived, which was her Uncle Jwe. Her mother was a single child but grew up with many close friends—Zaara's Moma grew up in an orphanage! She said that her father's parents died a year before Zaara was born. Zaara said that she would record the call for the judge and send it to her on the 2nd. Well, my hand hurts, and it is 9:00 p.m., so I am going to bed.

September

September 2nd

I did not write yesterday because I was busy preparing for the court date, which is tomorrow. Zaara sent the recording yesterday. My grandparents decided they were coming to the court with us, so they were super busy choosing their outfits. They needed help picking out their outfits, so I was running back and forth, helping all of them. Then I had to pick my outfit with Moma, then help her and my Doda pick theirs. After that, I took Mara on another walk with Moma, and we talked about what I would say. She said I should mention my feelings for Zaara, my work and hard plans to bring Zack to justice, and my connections to Ms. Singh and Ms. Joyce. Well, I have to go to bed now so I can be prepared for tomorrow.

September 3rd

Today we came back from court at 8:00 p.m. I want to first record what happened in court before I say what the judge decided.

Zack Burr, his lawyer (Noah Smith), Ms. Lucy Burr, Ms. Singh (our lawyer), Ms. Joyce, Moma, Doda, Nazzi Na, Nazzi Pa, Naja, and Paja all showed up. Judge Willow Williams kept a poker face the whole time, and called a break three times. Every time she called a break, Ms. Singh and Noah Smith went over to talk to her. But anyway, guess what the judge decided?! Zack Burr was... GUILTY! He will go to jail!

I called Zaara, and she was so excited that she screamed. It was really loud, so her aunt and uncle came to check on her. When they found out the good news, they screamed too! :) (I learned that symbol today from Ms. Singh, she said it is a sign of happiness. It looks like a happy face!) Moma and Doda were so excited. Nazzi Na and Naja fainted. Paja and Nazzi Pa had to wake them up! When we came home, Mara saw our happy faces and also got very excited.

School starts tomorrow, and I am going to get to share all this with my class!

September 4th

Today was my first day of school. It was so fun! I shared my family's story. All the other students were amazed about everything that my family went through and that I was there to tell it. My teacher asked about something special about me. I asked everyone if they knew about the court case that happened last night. A lot of them said yes. I asked them if they knew about Marie Altergott. I told them that was me! They all thought I was crazy and I wasn't really Marie Altergott. I told them that it was true, and Ms. Johnson, my teacher, confirmed it. I also met a really nice girl; Priscilla Beck. She is also German, I asked her. I also asked her if she would like to come over to my house, and she said yes! We walked home together. Moma and Doda were so happy I made a friend that they shouted happily and hugged me. They know I am very picky about choosing friends. And to choose someone of my origin is amazing for them.

The first thing my grandparents wanted to know was, since Priscilla was German; did her family support Hitler in World War II? I was so embarrassed that my grandparents asked that. She said that her family did not support Hitler and the Nazis. Paja and Nazzi Pa were very proud of that. They later told me never to make friends with Nazi supporters.
After Priscilla left, Naja said that I had made a great friend.

September 5th
Today, every student was supposed to share something about themselves in class that not everybody knew about them. I shared that I wrote in a journal almost every night and have recorded the absurd things that have happened in the last two or three months. I told my class, "A small amount of time might seem like ages, but going through what I went through and having a family story where my family perseveres and fights for what's right is how I have grown up. Fighting for what I fought for made that time go by so quickly. The times that hurt went by fast as well, and that was even worse, because they went by so quickly

that I had no time to address the wounds." After telling my class that, they looked at me like I said I met an Alien from Mars, so I said it in a more regular way: "My family has come from a long line of people who fought for what's right and persevered. The time that it took to bring me to America and solve a mystery went by so quickly. When I found out that Zaara, my best friend's parents were dead, it went by so quickly that I had no time to help Zaara heal and get over it." My teacher and class applauded. Ms. Johnson, my teacher, said that I should bring my journal down one day and let her look at it. I don't think so, Ms. Johnson.

Priscilla's mothers (she has two) came over tonight for dinner. We had Eintopf, which is, in our family, a fancy German stew. Both of Priscilla's mothers are bakers. I knew that from the beginning because her last name was Beck. They seemed very nice. I could tell that Priscilla was born here, but her mothers were not. That was one thing that seemed to draw a line between me and Priscilla: she was American-born; I was born in the UK. I was an immigrant, she was the daughter of immigrants. I think of it like this: When she has kids, they will be born American. My kids will be like Priscilla: born in the US. I told this to Moma. I was brought to America at the age of nine. I know that I have a different home country; it is different from being brought here at age one or two. That is a huge difference between me and Priscilla. But the funny thing is, I am not jealous of her. I am very proud to have come from another country. Another thing is, no matter where we both come from, I will always feel united with Priscilla because of our friendship.

I told Moma the reason I gravitated towards Zaara was because we had almost the same background. She is part English and part African. I am part English and part German. So, kind of like Priscilla and me. I guess none of us are so different after all. Zack Burr sure is, though. He is a villain in everyone's lives.

Now, I have to go to bed.

September 6th

Today was terrible!

Ms. Johnson is not very nice. She said that she ***understood!!*** why the Nazis did what they did. I already knew I was *not* going to let Ms. Johnson read my journal. I so badly wanted to raise my hand and tell her that the Nazis were wrong; what they did to humanity was *wrong.* In the end, I kept my mouth shut, but I kept thinking bad thoughts.

When I got home, Naja could see that something was wrong and brought Paja, Nazzi Na, and Nazzi Pa to come and check in on me. Paja could also see that something was wrong. I told them what Ms. Johnson had said. Naja and Paja were very mad, but Nazzi Pa was the maddest. He said that he was going to write a letter to my teacher. After he wrote it he gave it to me to give it to Ms. Johnson, but I threw it in our trash. I told Nazzi Na that I had thrown it away, and she said that she would tell Nazzi Pa when he had cooled down.

I talked to Moma and Doda, and they said not to get angry and just focus on proving my worth since I am Jewish.

Anyway, I am so proud that Nazzi Pa is the way he is and that he had freed the poor Jewish people in the German concentration camps.
Doda said that getting mad would just make Ms. Johnson angry and make her want to prove me wrong even more since she is the teacher, and I am just a student. Well, I can't write about it anymore, or else I will get just as mad as Nazzi Pa; and I do not want to have that part of him (no offense, Nazzi Pa).

September 7th
Today was okay; we kept learning about World War II. Thankfully, we moved off the unit on Nazis, and we are currently reading a book called The War That Saved My Life. It takes place in World War II, but the main character, Ada, does not know what World War II really is. The book is good, but I do not like the Ada. She is so unaware of a situation that affected my family. She was born in England, but she was not Jewish or German. I do not like her moma, either, because she treats Ada very rudely.

Priscilla was not here today, so I could not talk to her or play games with her at recess. All I did was read Who Was Alexander Hamilton? I finished that really quickly, so I got another book called Front Desk by Kelly Yang from my school library. The book is wonderful. It is about a girl who immigrated from China and works at a hotel, but she doesn't want to admit it to anyone. Well, here comes Nazzi Na and Naja to come and read me a bedtime story. Got to go.

September 8th

Today is Thursday, and today was a little boring. We had the day off of school. Because it was a Teacher work day. Priscilla called to tell me that the reason she was not there yesterday was because her family had gone up to Snow Town. They will be there till Sunday since we do not have school tomorrow either.

I played a lot of games with Naja and Paja, as well as took a lot of walks with Mara, Nazzi Na, and Nazzi Pa. I also read a lot of Front Desk today, and it was great! Moma and Doda love reading as well, so since we have a loft in our house, we all went up there to read today. It is about six feet in the air, so you have to climb a ladder to get there. Nazzi Pa and I had a race today. We each won two rounds, so since we had a tie to break and we each own a Rubik's Cube, we are having a challenge to see who can solve it first. (I am really close to solving it!) I am so excited for tomorrow because I am going to watch a documentary called Speed Cubers, which will teach me how to master the Rubik's Cube. Anyway, I am so tired, so I'm going to bed now.

September 9th
Sadly, this is the last page in my notebook. I have to stop writing in this notebook after this entry and buy a new notebook. But anyway, I watched the documentary and I mastered the Rubik's Cube! I beat Nazzi Pa! I told him I would this morning and he did not believe me, but I did! I am so proud of myself!
Well, goodbye, journal. I cannot wait to buy another journal and tell another story. I hope nothing bad happens next time around, but it seems like here in America and

everywhere else in the world, mistakes and terrible things happen. Something bad happened in the past few months, but I have fought through it and I can do it again as many more times as necessary.

I will miss you, journal. You have been something that has made me stronger. Even though I am stronger now, I will still get another journal and use it, and feel like I have reached the next level of strong training.

Author's Note

Hello readers,

First, I hope you all enjoyed my book *Life in America.* First of all, I am not from any German or Jewish or English origin.

I love this story because Marie shows something that I have always wanted to show: Strength, braveness, and barely any fear at all. When she does, she believes in herself to calm herself down. Marie is a great character who I try to make seem realistic.

Now, just so you know, everything I wrote about is not true. Marie's family story is not true, either. I wrote this story because, in a lot of books I have read, the world is perfect and everyone is equal. In real life, it is not, and that is the concept of my book. Marie and Zaara are both strong females. Nazzi Pa is modeled after my grandpa (Papa) who this book is dedicated to.

My grandpa is a big part of my life. He tells me stories about history and murder crimes—like this book.

Also, a shout out to Olivia Beck, a great friend. Her last name was used for Priscilla Beck.

I am currently ten years old. A lot of people that edited this book said I write like an adult. I did not write to show everyone this, though. I just wrote because I love writing.

I am starting to write another book. This is super exciting for me! I hope you'll stick around to read my next book.

Acknowledgements

And now, the acknowledgements.

First, Shannon Auxier for being a great family member and always asking questions that I hadn't thought about before. Shannon was always there. Once, she was on a forty-five minute phone call with me. She was a great help in creating this masterpiece. She is also a self-published author of *Khloe Can Be: A Police Officer.*

Elizabeth Johns is a friend of Shannon. She is also a published author. She filled out a form I used while writing this book and made some edits that made my book more appealing. She was a big help in writing my book, too.

Nadia Mustafa was my mother's past student. She looked at my story, asked some questions, and made me look at things from the point of view of a reader. Thank you!

Mora Ebie was able to get on a phone call with me to answer some questions. She is my cousin and the author of *Kai, The Honu Who Didn't Know He Was Brave.* She checked out my story and let me know how it looked. Mora was a great help.

Sarina Summers is the author of *Fedora's Secret.* I got in contact with her, and she made edits to my story; bringing things to my attention that I would never have noticed and that nobody had noticed up to this point. Thank you so much!

Abby Tsui & Canva helped come up with the cover. Abby was great help we got on a zoom, and she showed me some Canva designs. Then we found one and we settled on it. Without her there would be no cover.

Melissa Urizar is a middle school counselor but also a very close family friend. She asked great questions about how Zaara and Marie were feeling and made me think about adding little details that made great differences. Thank you!

Penny Warner was a great editor who helped my story appeal more to readers. She is also a published author of *The Code Buster Club* and other books. Having her edit my book made me feel proud. She became someone I was constantly emailing to ask her to check something or add an edit. Thank you!

Candace Whites is my mother, and was a huge help in publishing this book and making it into a true novel. Her commitment means a lot to me. She also helped pay to get this book self-published. Thank you!

Charles Whites is my dad. He paid for the ISBN which allowed me to publish my book, without him there would not be Life In America that you could read. I really want to thank him because like I said before if he had not paid for the ISBN there would be no Life In America.

Something I also want to do is thank myself for asking for edits and taking them to mind. I believed in myself and made something that I will always be proud of for years to come. Thank you!

Thank you to everyone who helped create, in my opinion, a masterpiece. And to all my readers, keep being strong, keep telling your story, and most importantly, keep being yourself. Embrace it!

Made in the USA
Monee, IL
04 November 2026

67383314R00037